AFRICA

by Madeline Donaldson

Lerner Publications Company • Minneapolis

Lerner Publications Company
A division of Lerner Publishing Group
241 First Avenue North
Minneapolis, MN 55401 U.S.A.

Website address: www.lernerbooks.com

Words in **bold type** are explained in a glossary on page 30.

Library of Congress Cataloging-in-Publication Data

Donaldson, Madeline.
    Africa / by Madeline Donaldson.
      p. cm. — (Pull ahead books)
    Summary: Introduces the continent of Africa and some of its unique characteristics. Includes bibliographical references and index.
    ISBN: 0–8225–4720–1 (lib. bdg. : alk. paper)
    1. Africa—Juvenile literature. [1. Africa.] I. Title.
    II. Series.
    DT3.D66 2005
    916–dc21   2003011216

Manufactured in the United States of America
1 2 3 4 5 6 – JR – 10 09 08 07 06 05

Photographs are used with the permission of: © Michele Burgess, pp. 3, 6–7, 8, 9, 11, 12, 15, 16, 18–19, 23, 26–27; © Jason Laure, pp. 10, 14, 21, 25; © Paul Joynson-Hicks, pp. 13, 17; © Jason Laure, p. 22; © John Vreyens, p. 24. Maps on pp. 4–5, 20, 29 by Laura Westlund.

Where could you sail along the world's longest river?

The **continent** of Africa! A continent is a big piece of land.

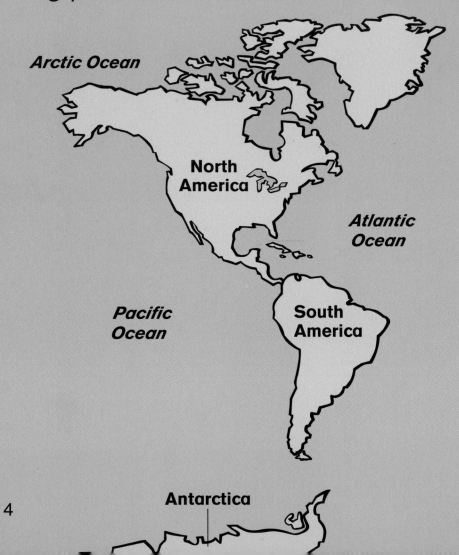

Arctic Ocean

North America

Atlantic Ocean

Pacific Ocean

South America

Antarctica

There are seven continents on Earth.
Four bodies of water surround Africa.

Arctic Ocean

Arctic Ocean

Europe

Asia

Mediterranean Sea

Red Sea

Africa

Pacific
Ocean

Indian
Ocean

Australia

Atlantic
Ocean

Antarctica

Africa has many different kinds of land.
Some land is for growing crops.

There are also grasslands, **deserts,** and forests in Africa.

Swish! Winds blow through this grassland. Africa's grasslands are called **savannas**. Can you name the animals in this savanna?

8

Sand covers Africa's deserts. The Sahara Desert is the largest desert in the world.

Plenty of rain falls in Africa's **tropical rain forests**. They spread across the middle of Africa.

Mountains tower over parts of Africa. Mount Kilimanjaro is Africa's tallest mountain.

Remember the longest river? It is called the Nile River. It runs for thousands of miles.

The Nile starts in Lake Victoria.
Victoria is the biggest lake in Africa.
People fish for food in Lake Victoria.

Hundreds of kinds of plants are found in Africa. These baobab trees grow in the savannas.

Yum! Sweet, sticky dates come from
date palm trees in Africa's deserts.

Many kinds of animals live in Africa.
These hippos cool themselves in a river.

A shy gorilla seeks a hiding place in a tropical rain forest.

More than eight hundred million people
live in Africa. They belong to hundreds
of **ethnic groups**.

The people in an ethnic group may share the same language and the same religion.

Africa has five **regions.** The regions are North Africa, West Africa, East Africa, Central Africa, and Southern Africa.

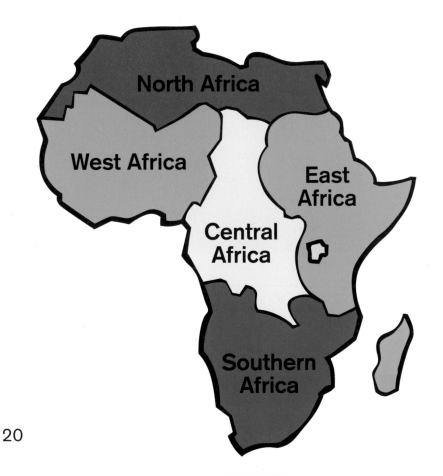

Many North Africans are Arab. Most
Arabs follow a religion called Islam.
This man from Morocco is getting
ready to pray.

Nigeria is the largest country in West Africa. The region's biggest city is Lagos, Nigeria.

The Masai people live in East Africa.
Masai girls wear colorful clothing.

Pound, pound, pound! Women in Congo,
Central Africa, make flour by hand.

Gold mining takes place in Southern Africa. This miner is drilling into rock.

Africa has many interesting places! Do you know about the pyramids?

They were built as **tombs** for kings and queens in Egypt, North Africa.

There's always something new to learn about Africa!

Cool Facts about Africa

- Africa covers more than 11 million square miles (28.5 million square kilometers).

- The main rivers of Africa are the Nile River, the Congo River, the Niger River, and the Zambezi River.

- Some of the animals of Africa are camels, crocodiles, elephants, giraffes, hippos, impalas, lions, and ostriches.

- Elephant grasses and papyrus are two kinds of plants that grow in Africa.

- More than eight hundred million people live in Africa.

- People in Africa follow Islam, Christianity, and traditional religions.

Map of Africa

Tunisia
Morocco
Western Sahara
Algeria
Libya
Egypt
Mauritania
Senegal
Mali
Niger
Eritrea
Djibouti
Gambia
Chad
Sudan
Guinea-Bissau
Somalia
Guinea
Ethiopia
Sierra Leone
Nigeria
Liberia
Ivory Coast
Benin
Uganda
Togo
Kenya
Ghana
Rwanda
Gabon
Burundi
Congo
Malawi
Tanzania
Angola
Zambia
Namibia
Madagascar
Botswana
Mozambique
South Africa
Zimbabwe
Swaziland
Lesotho

Ⓐ Burkina Faso
Ⓑ Cameroon
Ⓒ Equatorial Guinea
Ⓓ Central African Republic
Ⓔ Democratic Republic of the Congo

Glossary

continent: one of seven big pieces of land on Earth. Africa is the second largest continent, after Asia.

deserts: hot areas that don't get much rain.

ethnic groups: people who have many things in common. They might speak the same language or follow the same religion.

regions: small parts of a larger piece of land

savannas: the grasslands of Africa

tombs: places that hold a dead body

tropical rain forests: green forests that get a lot of rain throughout the year

Further Reading and Websites

Foster, Leila Merrell. *Africa.* Crystal Lake, IL: Heinemann Library, 2001.

Fowler, Allan. *Africa.* Danbury, CT: Children's Press, 2002.

Harvey, Miles. *Look What Came from Africa.* Danbury, CT: Franklin Watts, 2002.

Littlefield, Holly. *Colors of Ghana.* Minneapolis: Carolrhoda Books, Inc., 1999.

McCollum, Sean. *Kenya.* Minneapolis: Carolrhoda Books, Inc., 1999.

Nelson, Robin. *Where Is My Continent?* Minneapolis: Lerner Publications Company, 2002.

Oluonye, Mary N. *Nigeria.* Minneapolis: Carolrhoda Books, Inc., 1998.

Oluonye, Mary N. *South Africa.* Minneapolis: Carolrhoda Books, Inc., 1999.

Sammis, Fran. *Colors of Kenya.* Minneapolis: Carolrhoda Books, Inc., 1998.

Sayre, April Pulley. *Good Morning, Africa!* Brookfield, CT: Millbrook Press, 2003.

Streissguth, Tom. *Egypt.* Minneapolis: Carolrhoda Books, Inc., 1999.

Enchanted Learning
<http://enchantedlearning.com/geography/africa>
The geography section of this website has links to every continent.

Kids' Africa
<http://www.pbs.org/wonders/kids/kids>
This is part of the website that goes with the PBS program, *Wonders of the African World.* The site features crafts, stories, and other activities.

Index